Those Lively Lizards

Argentine black
and white tegu

Marta Magellan

Illustrated by Steve Weaver

Photographs by James Gersing

Pineapple Press, Inc.

Sarasota, Florida

Photo Credits
Photographs by James Gersing except: red-headed agama by Johann Axelsson, basilisk lizard by Christopher Russell, crested gecko hatching by James VanZetta—all three from istockphoto; green iguana with half tail in Pantanal, Brazil, by Marta Magellan

Inquiries should be addressed to:

Pineapple Press, Inc.
P.O. Box 3889
Sarasota, Florida 34230

www.pineapplepress.com

Library of Congress Cataloging-in-Publication Data

Magellan, Marta
Those lively lizards / Marta Magellan ; photographs by James Gersing.-- 1st ed.
p. cm.
Includes bibliographical references and index.
ISBN-13: 978-1-56164-426-1 (hardback : alk. paper)
ISBN-13: 978-1-56164-427-8 (pbk. : alk. paper)
1. Lizards--Juvenile literature. I. Gersing, James, ill. II. Title.
QL666.L2M24 2008
597.95--dc22
2008008932

First Edition
Hb 10 9 8 7 6 5 4 3 2 1
Pb 10 9 8 7 6 5 4 3 2 1

Design by Steve Weaver
Printed in China

To Sophie, Leia, Rachel, and Julia

Special thanks to:

Dr. Larry Wilson, tropical herpetologist and professor at Miami Dade College for evaluating the manuscript.

We are also grateful to: Tamian Wood for designing and Mauro Magellan for illustrating the activities; Linda Bernfeld along with all the members of the Miami SCWBI critique group for their suggestions, and Tracy Monique Magellan for assisting with photography.

Also essential to the photographs in the book: Emily Krapf and her friendly bearded dragons Kevin and Drew, Noel Walter, Mike Barrera from Snakes at Sunset, and the many friendly zookeepers at Miami Metro Zoo.

Contents

Green iguana

What are lizards?

Lizards are part of a large group of reptiles, a class of animals with mostly dry, horny scales. This group includes iguanas, chameleons, geckos, monitors, and skinks. Many of them can leap, climb trees, and swim. One even runs on water! Some of them look like little dinosaurs. Others are like little alligators. Some even remind you of fierce storybook dragons. A long time ago, when people saw lizards like the bearded dragon, they thought they were baby dragons! There are over 4,500 species (types) of lizards in the world. Bet you can't name them all!

Red-headed agama

Why are lizards important?

Lizards are both predator and prey. This means they eat and are eaten by other animals. As predators, lizards eat many insects. They are like nature's pest controllers. They are also prey because other animals need to eat lizards to stay alive. Many birds, small mammals, snakes, and even the larger lizards depend on having plenty of lizards to eat. Some people in Mexico and Central America catch iguanas for food. They call them *pollo de palo* (chicken of the tree). They think they're yummy.

Komodo dragon

Anole

How big are lizards?

Lizards come in all sizes. The smallest one is the dwarf gecko. It is so tiny you can hold it on the tip of your finger. You can hold the knob-tailed gecko in the palm of your hand. You have to use two hands to hold a grown blue-tongued skink. Don't try to hold a Komodo dragon! It's the largest lizard of all. It can grow up to ten feet (three meters) long. That's as big as an alligator! Wouldn't it be funny if a Komodo dragon and a little anole were friends?

Green iguanas

Where do lizards live?

Lizards can be found almost everywhere. They make their homes mostly on the ground, but several live in trees. The marine iguana spends a lot of its time in the water. Skinks and glass lizards live in underground burrows. That's why they have short legs or none at all. There are lizards living in the hottest deserts and in the wettest rainforests. Lizards don't like the super cold places, so you won't find any at the North Pole (or the South Pole, either).

Green iguana

How do lizards escape?

Lizards have many ways to escape. Usually they run away fast (sometimes on their hind legs). They can also freeze to blend into their surroundings. When chased or bitten, a lizard can shed its tail on purpose like the iguana in the photograph did. A few lizards try to scare the predator. The frill-necked lizard makes a ruff around its neck flare out. Others puff up their bodies to look bigger. Some horned lizards squirt blood from their eyes to startle their attacker!

Anole

Can a lizard's tail really grow back?

When a lizard's tail is bitten, it snaps off. Ouch! There are special places in the tail where it can make a clean break. Sometimes the separated tail wiggles to distract the predator. When it grows back, the tail won't ever be as big as it once was. That's still better for the lizard than being a hungry animal's snack!

Veiled chameleon

Knight anole

Is it true lizards change colors to match their surroundings?

The colors on a lizard can change with the lizard's mood (scared, angry), outside temperature (hot, cold) and with the amount of darkness or light. Anoles are a type of lizard that can change from bright green to brown (see the photo insets). Chameleons are lizards that can change to many different colors and patterns to blend with what is around them (called camouflage). But even chameleons can't match every surrounding. If you put a chameleon on a plaid bedspread, it's not going to turn plaid!

changing room

21

Madagascar day
gecko

What's a gecko?

A gecko is a type of lizard that can walk on glass windows and upside down on ceilings because of its broad, bristly toes. Other lizards would fall right off if they tried it. Some geckos have special eyes so they can hunt in the dark—unlike most lizards, who hunt for food during the day. A gecko can make sounds like chirping, squeaking, or clicking. On spring and summer evenings the tokay gecko yells out "Uh-oh!" Other kinds of lizards aren't noisy like that.

Jackson's
chameleon

Why do some lizards look like little dinosaurs?

They look alike because both lizards and dinosaurs are reptiles. The word dinosaur comes from the Greek meaning "terrible lizard." Some lizards can run on their hind legs like *Tyrannosaurus rex*. Others have horns like *Triceratops*. Iguanas have been used many times in Hollywood movies to stand in for dinosaurs. A frilled lizard was used as a model for a *Jurassic Park* dinosaur, and a Komodo dragon was the model for Godzilla the lizard monster.

Marble gecko

Do lizards bite?

Lizards will sometimes bite if you handle them. Their bite can make you bleed, but it won't make you sick. Two lizards have dangerous bites: the Mexican beaded lizard and the Gila (pronounced hee-la) monster. If they bite you, it will hurt a lot (but you probably won't die). Komodo dragons have lots of bacteria in their mouths. An animal bitten by a Komodo may die later from an infection.

WARNING ATTACK LIZARD!

Crested gecko

How are lizards born?

Most lizards hatch from an egg. Some types of lizards give birth to living baby lizards. When lizards lay eggs, it is usually on the ground in hidden places, like under a rotting log or in between the roots of trees. Depending on the type of lizard it is, it can lay one egg or lots of eggs. Lizard eggs can stretch as the baby lizard inside grows. When the baby lizard is ready to come out of the egg, it cuts its way out with a sharp egg tooth. The tooth drops off later. Too bad lizards don't get visits from tooth fairies!

Anole

What do baby lizards look like?

Baby lizards look like tiny adult lizards when they hatch. They start running around the minute they hatch. Lizard mothers aren't really very good mothers. Except for some skinks, lizard mothers usually don't hang around after they lay their eggs. Fortunately, the baby lizards are just like adult lizards. They know how to survive (stay alive) right after hatching.

Goodbye. Have a nice life. Love, Mom

Green iguana

Do lizards shed their skins like snakes?

The scaly skin on a lizard doesn't grow with its body, so a lizard needs to shed (or molt) its skin. Lizards have all kinds of scales. Skinks, for example, have very smooth skin. The desert iguana is very scaly. The Gila monster has scales that look like beads. But they all have to shed. Snakes tend to slither out of their skins, but lizards shed in patches. When they shed, new skin is already underneath the old skin, so they don't feel naked.

Bearded dragon

What do lizards eat?

Most lizards prefer insects like crickets, grasshoppers, and even flies. Yuck! Others like snails, slugs, worms, or mice. Double yuck! Many lizards like fruit and eggs, and others prefer flowers, leaves, and plants of all kinds. Then there are the Komodo dragons. They eat anything. They can hunt and kill large mammals like deer or cows! They rarely attack people, but it can happen, so don't get too close! They don't mind eating stuff that's already dead, either. They can smell a dead animal from as far away as six miles (ten kilometers).

Knob-tailed
gecko

Why do some lizards have funny-looking eyes?

Lizards have very special eyes because they need to hunt, escape from predators, and do many other things. Iguanas see in color and use color to communicate with each other. Night geckos have big catlike eyes. They hunt at night and need to see in the dark. The slits in their eyes will open up to let as much light in as possible.

The funniest lizard eyes belong to chameleons. Both eyes can look in different directions— up, down, all around. It's no use trying to sneak up on them!

**Blue-tongued
skink**

Why do lizards stick out their tongues?

Tongues are super important to lizards. Blue-tongued skinks stick their tongues out when they feel threatened. That can really scare an attacker! Chameleons have long, sticky tongues that can grab an insect really fast. Geckos need their tongues to lick their eyeballs! They don't have eyelids, so licking keeps their eyes moist and clean. You'll be surprised to know that lizards smell with their tongues! They use smell to recognize mates, enemies, and food.

Veiled chameleon

Can a lizard be a pet?

Many lizards can get used to people if they are handled gently when they are young. Some lizards never want to be touched, but people keep them for their unusual looks. The bearded dragon is a good pet. In spite of its fierce name, it is actually quite sweet. It will let you hold it and it will sit on your lap for hours. A lizard that is easy to take care of is the leopard gecko, but *all* pet lizards need lots of special care.

Anole

Do boy and girl lizards look the same?

In many cases, boy (male) and girl (female) lizards look alike, but the male is a bit bigger. There are some species with big differences. Rainbow lizard males have brighter colors than females. The male Jackson's chameleon has horns on its head, but the female doesn't. The male anole has a colorful fan that comes out of his throat, called a dewlap. He sticks out the dewlap to show off to a female or to scare off anybody who threatens him.

Basilisk lizard

Which lizard runs on water?

The basilisk lizards of the Central American rainforests are called the Jesus Christ lizards because they can walk (actually run) on water! When you ride your bike, you will fall if you don't keep moving. The lizard must keep running to stay on top of the water. If you want to see one crossing a stream on its hind legs, go to the back of the book where a website link will show you a video clip of one doing just that.

Malayan water monitor

Are lizards endangered?

Many species of lizards are threatened throughout the world. That's because many of the areas they live in are being used for people. The Komodo dragon lives only on four small islands in Indonesia. The green iguana is threatened because in some places people eat them and their eggs. Still, many lizards do quite well even around people. For example, the Malayan water monitor continues to survive in spite of losing a lot of living space. It's a good thing there are still a lot of lizards. We need them to keep the balance of nature.

Lizard crossword puzzle

Directions: Answer the clues to finish the crossword puzzle.

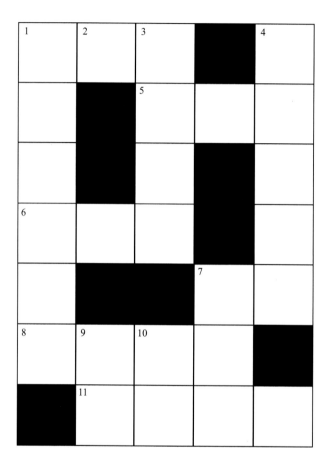

Across:
  1. A baby cat is a ____ ten.
  5. What the lizard did when he was hungry
  6. Something to put on salads or in car motors
  7. You ask to take home food by asking for it __ go.
  8. Upon or on top of
  11. Not closed

Down:
  1. _____ dragon
  2. Me, myself, and _____
  3. What drops off a lizard when it's chased?
  4. Big-eyed lizard that can walk on walls
  7. Part of your foot
  9. Opposite of yes
  10. These two letters together sound like a Native American tent.

To reveal the answers turn this page upside down and look at it in a mirror.

48

Follow the numbers chameleon

Directions: Photocopy the page. Beginning with number one follow the numbers until a chameleon appears.

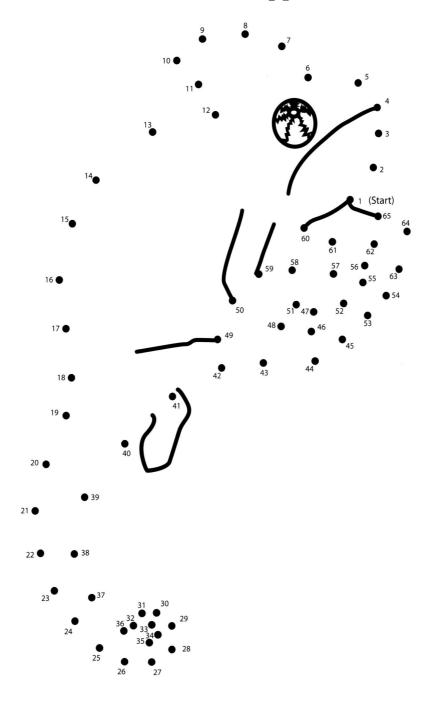

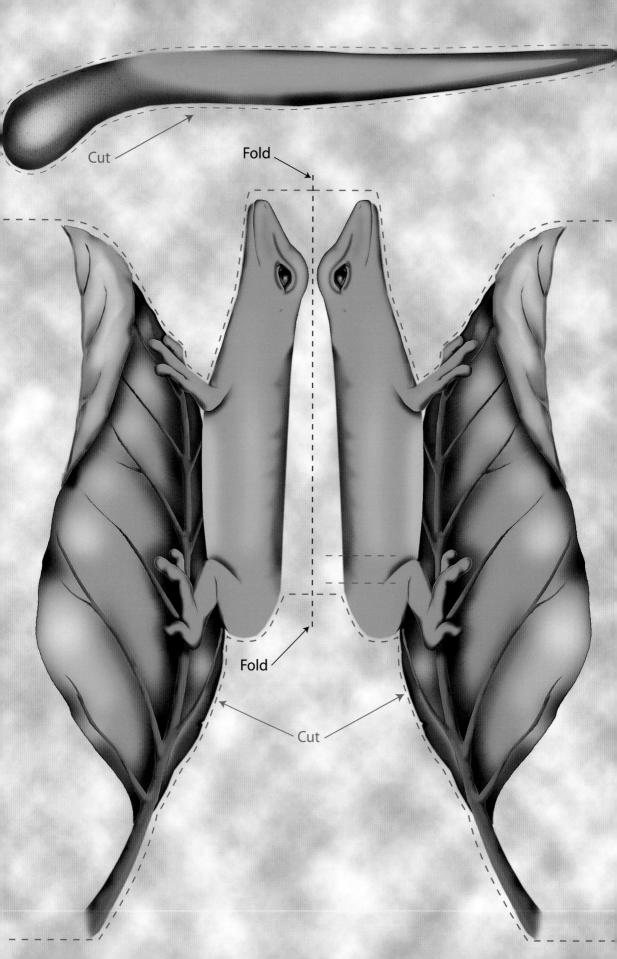

Cut

Fold

Fold

Cut

Anole puppet

Materials Needed
- card stock
- glue stick
- sharp blade
- 3 craft sticks
- scissors

1. Copy illustration onto card stock to give your lizard some strength.
2. Cut carefully along the red dotted lines of the tail piece.
3. Glue a craft stick to the back of the tail piece.
4. Cut carefully along the red dotted lines of the lizard.
5. Glue a craft stick to each inside bottom edge (for strength)
6. Have an adult help you cut the slits on the back of the lizard with a sharp blade.
7. Slide the tail piece into the cut slits.
8. Fold along the black dotted line.

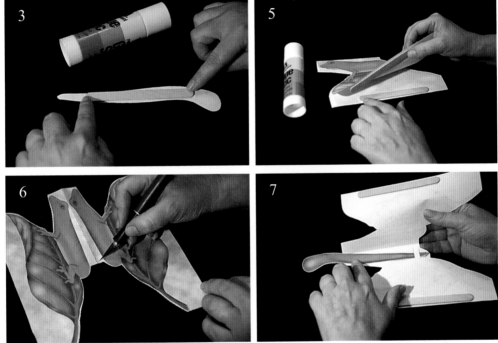

Slide the tail up and down to see the Anole lizard display his dewlap.

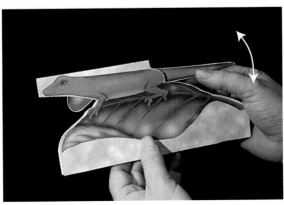

Glossary

camouflage – skin colors that blend in with the surroundings

captivity – living inside a limited area like a cage or a house; not in the wild

carnivores – animals that eat meat

endangered – animals in danger of becoming extinct; not many left in the wild

monitor – a type of carnivorous (meat-eating) lizard

predators – animals that kill other animals for food

scavengers – animals that eat whatever they can find, including dead animals

species – a particular kind of plant or animal

surroundings – things that are around you

survive – to stay alive

threatened – likely to become endangered, fewer and fewer left in the wild

Where to learn more about lizards

Books

- Arnosky, Jim. *All About Lizards.* New York: Scholastic Inc. Scholastic, 2004.
- Badger, David. *Lizards: A Natural History of Some Uncommon Creatures—Extraordinary Chameleons, Iguanas, Geckos, and More.* Minnesota: MBI Publishing, Voyageur Press, 2006.
- Holub, Joan. *Why Do Snakes Hiss? And Other Questions about Snakes, Lizards, and Turtles.* New York: Penguin Young Readers Group, Puffin Books, 2004.

Websites

- www.sandiegozoo.org/animalbytes/t-lizard.html
- www.isidore-of-seville.com/komodo
- www.geckolist.com
- http://animal-world.com/encyclo/reptiles/information/lizardclassfamilies

- To hear some gecko sounds go to Global Gecko Association: www.gekkota.org/html/gecko_sounds.html
- To see a Jesus Christ lizard walking across water: video.google.com/videoplay?docid=9005492250163913372

About the author

Marta Magellan is a nature lover who teaches English, Creative Writing, and Survey of Children's Literature at Miami Dade College. An avid admirer of wildlife, she travels often to Brazil and wherever else she can find a wilderness. She lives in Miami, Florida, with her husband, James Gersing, the photographer for this book.

Index

(Numbers in **bold** refer to photographs.)

Here are the other books in this series. For a complete catalog, write to Pineapple Press, P.O. Box 3889, Sarasota, Florida 34230-3889, or call (800) 746-3275. Or visit our website at www.pineapplepress.com.

Those Amazing Alligators by Kathy Feeney. Illustrated by Steve Weaver, photographs by David M. Dennis. Alligators are amazing animals, as you'll see in this book. Discover the differences between alligators and crocodiles; learn what alligators eat, how they communicate, and much more. Ages 5–9.

Those Beautiful Butterflies by Sarah Cussen. Illustrated by Steve Weaver. This book answers 20 questions about butterflies—their behavior, why they look the way they do, how they communicate, and much more. Ages 5–9.

Those Delightful Dolphins by Jan Lee Wicker. Illustrated by Steve Weaver. Learn the difference between a dolphin and a porpoise, find out how dolphins breathe and what they eat, and learn how smart they are and what they can do. Ages 5–9.

Those Excellent Eagles by Jan Lee Wicker. Illustrated by Steve Weaver, photographs by H. G. Moore III. Learn all about those excellent eagles—what they eat, how fast they fly, why the American bald eagle is our nation's national bird. You'll even make some edible eagles. Ages 5–9.

Those Funny Flamingos by Jan Lee Wicker. Illustrated by Steve Weaver. Flamingos are indeed funny birds. Learn why those funny flamingos are pink, stand on one leg, eat upside down, and much more. Ages 5–9.

Those Magical Manatees by Jan Lee Wicker. Illustrated by Steve Weaver. Twenty questions and answers about manatees—you'll find out more about their behavior, why they're endangered, and what you can do to help. Ages 5–9.

Those Outrageous Owls by Laura Wyatt. Illustrated by Steve Weaver, photographs by H. G. Moore III. Learn what owls eat, how they hunt, and why they look the way they do. You'll find out what an owlet looks like, why horned owls have horns, and much more. Ages 5–9.

Those Peculiar Pelicans by Sarah Cussen. Illustrated by Steve Weaver, photographs by Roger Hammond. Find out how much food those peculiar pelicans can fit in their beaks, how they stay cool, and whether they really steal fish from fishermen. And learn how to fold up an origami pelican. Ages 5–9.

Those Terrific Turtles by Sarah Cussen. Illustrated by Steve Weaver, photographs by David M. Dennis. You'll learn the difference between a turtle and a tortoise, and find out why they have shells. Meet baby turtles and some very, very old ones, and even explore a pond. Ages 5–9.

Those Voracious Vultures by Marta Magellan. Illustrated by Steve Weaver, photographs by James Gersing and Ron Magill. Learn all about vultures—the gross things they do, what they eat, whether a turkey vulture gobbles, and more. Ages 5–9.